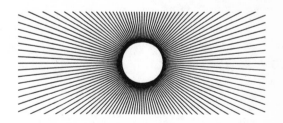

Pottersfield Press

BORROWED BEAUTY

Maxine Tynes

Pottersfield Press, Porters Lake, Nova Scotia, Canada

FOR MY MOTHER, ADA MAXWELL-TYNES

Canadian Cataloguing in Publication Data
Tynes, Maxine
  Borrowed beauty

Poems.
ISBN 0-919001-38-6

I. Title.

PS8589.Y64B67   1987   C811'.54   C87-093692-1
PR9199.3.T96B67   1987

Some of these works have previously appeared in *Fireweed, Other Voices, New Maritimes, The Pottersfield Portfolio,* and on CBC radio.

Cover photo: Albert Lee
Book design: Lesley Choyce
Typesetting: Dal Graphics

Published with the support of the Nova Scotia Department of Culture, Recreation and Fitness

Fourth Printing 1992
Reprint assistance provided by the Canada Council

Contents

Mirrors

Women are always looking into mirrors, looking for a mirror to look into, or thinking about, regretting, sighing over or not quite believing what they've seen in the mirror.

We're looking at ourselves; looking for ourselves. The girls we were, the women we are, and what we will become. Searching, always searching in mirrors.

For people of colour, for Black people, for this Black woman in particular, the search is the same, but different. We are constantly looking for who we are. So many of the signals have been lost, historically and culturally, along the way.

I'm (at least) a fourth generation Black Canadian woman, writer, poet, broadcast journalist, teacher, performance artist. But as soon as I say something in print or otherwise about my Black past I have to qualify it; because we as a people have lost many tangible, documented traces of who we are.

I cannot possibly say to you that I am a woman descendent from the people of the plains — the Serengeti, of Kenya, of Ghana, the Gambia or of

Zaire — the heartland. I can only look to the vast expanse of Africa, that black mother continent, and say, that is who and what and where I am.

For me, a Black woman four generations hence on these shores, that is a lament into the mirror of the map of that place. Africa.

Or, I can, as I sometimes do, look into my mother's face. And, seeing she has the high, proud nose of North Africa, I wonder about the where —the valley, the tribal name, the kinship and origins I will never know. That, too, is a lament.

Then, as I often do, I look into my poet's soul to find there the route to self and personhood, both Black and female. That looking is not a lament but the greatest of joys.

My poems, my poetry are like mirrors reflecting back in great or subtle beams and shafts of light and words and images that are womanly and Black and brown and tan and full of the joy and pride in femaleness and in Black womanhood that I am.

My poems are great shouts of the joy that I feel and share; the deep passion that rocks and caresses and embraces me and all that is part of my world and my life. The laments for lost heritage are there; but, then, so are the feelings of having found a centre and a self-acceptance and an identity in this Black and woman's skin that I so joyfully wear.

I wear it joyfully. I wear it big. I wear it womanly. And I wear it Black. Black. Black. As night, deep and soft and endless with no moon. Just black and perfect splendour in life and in being a woman in this world.

Womanskin

women
we keepers and sharers of ancient secrets
of loving
and making homes of houses
of loving
and making love
of loving
and making life
of loving
and making our men whole
of loving
and being women, wives, mothers sisters, daughters, lovers,
strong, aunts, free, grandmothers, constant, nieces,
women, and Black
we women of colour
distant daughters of
the Nile, the Sahara, Kenya, Zaire, Sudan
the Serengeti
we dance the body-music of light and shadow
we share the palette spectrum
the obsidian sunshade
burnished blue-black brown tantan sepia
coffeecoffee cream ebony
delight of womanskin
strong in
alive in
free in
loving in

working in
laughing in
sharing in
mothering in
growing in
aging in
this skin
this night shade of many shades
this womanskin
we women
keepers and sharers of ancient secrets.

In Service

This poem is dedicated to the generations of Black women who sustained life and survival for their families by bending low in labour in generations of white kitchens.

Saturday morning armies
of Black women
young
and old
and, young and old at the same time
in the same face
in the same care and time and work-worn hands
you rise with the dawn
leaving home and brown babies
behind you, in the day's early light
pulling coat and scarf close
avoiding the mirror
shrinking from the cold morning of
bus ride
to prestigious street corner.

you are not alone
you are with your sisters in this
Northend - to Southend
Jane Finch - to Rosedale
Montreal - to Outremont
Harlem - to Scarsdale
wearing head-rag
carrying dust-mop, scrub-bucket
in-service three days a week march in the dawn.

you possess a key, cherished girl (never woman) of this house
you tap and scuffle and wipe feet at the back
and enter the world of
day's
day's
day's work in service
taking your place in that army of
round and strong and weary backs
moving with grace and sure familiar stride
from your kitchen
your babies
your own forgotten morning at home
to this
three days-a-week armies of Black women
in service.

For Linda

us meeting
after months
embrace in people/smoke/talk-crowded
Bay Boy premier reception room
' my cancer has come back ' you said
so everyday ordinary strong
like a change of address card
but your eyes were blazing, fevered,
too bright with cancer and anger
me stupid
    shocked
    stupid
you, my first brush/touch up close with this

later
you, died
I answered the phone
        said things
I did not witness your funeral

later, still
some people/smoke/talk-crowded
film-media pow - wow room
me, meeting your woman — partner in film
we embrace for you
she whispers in my ear
' I have a message for you from Linda '

whispered words of your childhood memories
a Black nannie's warm arms
so big and brown around you
like mine
around you that crowded *Bay Boy* night
when you said
' it's back.'

Hollis Street at Midnight is not a T.V. Screen

Hollis Street at midnight is not a T.V. screen
is not riding the bus at 8:00 a.m. to some safe office
is not choosing nail polish
to match your image
after having your colours done
is not a cute middle-class, new man / new woman
cerebral struggle of
who will pay the cheque
who will insist on a fifty-fifty nouveau-egalitarian split
who will tally the tip with mean precision
and how many orgasmic points are won or lost over that issue
- multiple, or otherwise

is not a daytime soap lethargic eclipse of flickering dream-images
which take you into a twenty minute workout of
leftovers, or
hibachi cook-out in some loft
or take-out

is not high-noon Spring Garden Road well-dressed, khaki-clad
biological imperative sisterhood/non-sisterhood
I-am-not-a-feminist-BUT elite
sitting on the wall eating Bud The Spud
and having affordable cellulite fantasies

Hollis Street at midnight
is women walking their blues
in the night of men walking their blues
in the night of women and shadows

the collision of currency and flesh and middle-class community
    angst
Hollis Street at midnight is not a T.V. screen.

For Salome

(Written for Salomé Bey, writer of the anti-apartheid song, "Family Called Mankind" and for all of us: the singers of the song against apartheid; May 10, 1986 in Toronto for the Anti-apartheid Festival.)

on this day, Uitenhage,
we sing for you
and your bloody dead
on this Toronto day
we sing for you
against apartheid
Winnie, can you hear us?
we sing
we sing
we sing
in some old cathedral
voices of men and women
chasing devils
we sing
Salome's song of peace
               family
             man
and the family of man/womankind

how easily equality rises in our throats
slips up and up and up
like a lyrical flag

Was it another party for the press?
Was it a song you could sing, Winnie?
                              or, Nelson?
or poor lost and bloodied bodies of Sharpville
                              of Soweto
                              of Jo'burg

on this day, Uitenhage
            Jo'burg
            Sharpville
Winnie and Nelson
through Salome, we sing for you.

Speaking Our Peace

To the film SPEAKING OUR PEACE;
to the energy of the women who made it;
and to the energy of the audience we are
when we see this film; and to the power of peace it
gives to us.

SPEAKING OUR PEACE
alone
and together
speaking our peace
speaking our peace
film-flicker of women
living in the war of peacetime
speaking our peace
Marian Dewar
Muriel Duckworth
Bonnie Klein
Terri Nash
Dr. Ursula Franklin
Rosalie Bertell
Kathleen Wallace-Deering
Darlene Keju
Solanges Vincent
Margaret Laurence
and all of us
women
and, men and women
and children
speaking our peace

to see people of colour
not just as victims of colour
in a newsreel
in a war
in a film
speaking our peace
trading future lives
for now-jobs in the war machine
in heavy water
and gas masks
and anchors for
nuclear submarines
fuel rods
and PCB-filled railway cars
speaking our peace
sitting elbow-to-elbow in the dark of
1985 Halifax Women's Peace Conference room
sharing fears of the nuclear night
              the nuclear day
              the nuclear winter nightmare
that we live through now
here
today
this night
speaking our peace
recognizing and
pushing back the fear
and the reality of living in
the global battle field

living in the war in peacetime
living in the war in peacetime
living in the war in peacetime

SPEAKING OUR PEACE
SPEAKING OUR PEACE
SPEAKING OUR PEACE.

Avec Mes Soeurs
Con Mis Hermanas
With My Sisters

This poem is for Vilma Nunez de Escorcia.
This poem is for the women, the children,
the families of Nicaragua.
This poem is for the women, the children,
the families of the world who are united in the struggle for peace.

your words of blood and
struggle
rise and root like trees
in our collective auditorium
hearts and minds
this peace conference night
sitting
plush and comfortable
as your words fall like knives
we, too, are Nicaraguan
as you draw for us
a map of your homeland
in pain
we, too, are Nicaraguan
as the village children
run wild to hide in their
fear of gunsounds
at dawn
   dusk
   midnight

we, too, are Nicaraguan
as you trade your cookstove
and your marriage bed
for small arms
and hillside skirmishes
beside your man
wishing in your heart
crying in your sleep
to instead be in his arms
and he in yours
then, we too, are Nicaraguan
as we shop for meat
and sweet, fresh Canadian milk
as you feed your children the tough talk
borne of motherhood practised, and well-versed in
womanhood with hands on the war
in seeing you thus
we, too, are Nicaraguan
as we turn on our t.v.
and in the nightly litany
of Grenada
   Beirut
   Uitenhage
   Johannesburg
   Nicaragua
as the bodies fall into our livingrooms
as we colour our hair
as we play and dress for each other
as we try on for size being
women
wives
friends

mothers
activists
lovers
witnesses of your struggle
victims of our own North American-isms
in all of this; we, too, are Nicaraguan
Vilma Nunez de Escorcia
you
we
and all of us
women,
living in the war in peacetime.

Womanquest

reaching out and
reaching in
to all the women
that we are
to all the women
that we could be.
What of the woman
who is Black, and reaching?
What of the woman
who is poor, and homeless?
What of the woman
who is Native, and of the First People?
What of the woman
who is battered, and hurting?
there is room and time and
place for all of these women
that we are
down all the corridors
of power
and rank
and privilege
and place.
me,
wondering
looking
seeking.
you,
in corporate

or industrial
or political splendour
doing the dance
in and out and in again
of all of our isms
borrowed a male and useless dance
around colour and issues and studies
all of that well-documented and establishment doublespeak
that says: wait,
        go slow
        step back
no time or money for you now
when a clear voice
is all that I want
a clear and equal
and true vision
to bridge the differences
to make us whole
and women
and strong
and women
and learned
and women
and sharing as women
to heal the body politic.

Live Aid in a Basket: The Reach Out and Touch Fantasy of the Century

it felt more honest
in '68
in '72
in '75
to march in parks
trailing flowers and beads
and some virile, corn-fed American draft dodger
kissing behind placards
and singing free Bobby (Seale)
        free Angela (Davis)
        free women
        free Vietnam
now
fat and complacent
with one finger on the t.v. trigger
we sit in our livingrooms
and think we are freeing the world
we free Africa/Ethiopia
Live! and in living Bruce Springsteen, Mick Jagger and
Stevie Wonder soul/blues/rock opera colour.

I watched it, too
this rock/t.v./satellite media event of the decade.

What is the equation
for some black and hunger-shrivelled woman, child
bag of bones in rags and dust Ethiopia?
Does one Bob Dylan revival
equal one bowl of infested rice and protein supplement?

pass the pizza and beer during the commercial
freeze-frame Bowie and Jagger mid-prance
save it for later

How does that earth-brown mother with flapping breasts
like envelopes save her starvation for later?
What does it matter?
multiplied by camera and reality,
she is such a natural and constant photo opportunity.

somebody should take a poll;
What were you doing during LIVE AID?
was it party, party, party time
all over the western world?
Did you order in take-out?
Did you have your beer on ice?
Did you program the V.C.R.?
Did you make love between sets?

it felt more honest in '72.
What 1985 save-the-world memories will you tell your grandkids?
how you marched from the fridge to the t.v. during the
world wide THE WHO t.v. revival, but sat
glued and thrilled to death during the Jagger/Bowie number
And as for Jagger and Tina Turner,
that leather-to-leather song and dance number

did more to raise eyebrows, and sagging libidos
than it did to raise the survival quotient
in some desert village that none of us can pronounce the name of
or wants to, anyway...

And where in the blue and flickering t.v. world
is Ethiopia now?
in the ratings war, terrorism is 10 Neilson points
above world aid for hunger.

so; save the cover from LIFE magazine
learn the lyrics of WE ARE THE WORLD
have a LIVE AID video party
and seduce your next lover by chanting the names of

all the singers in alphabetical order
with the lights out.

not quite what Bob Geldoff had in mind
but close enough.

this is THE 80s.
everything is freeze-dried instant
now
now
now
more; much more

and anyway,
if we can't handle it,
the Third World can come and save us.

Becoming Rita

for Rita MacNeil
from Big Pond, Cape Breton

Rita
when you sing
we all become Cape Bretoners
hearts underground
workingmen
miners
and grandmother's knee is right there
                         right there
some smokey night in the L.B.R.
as "The Working Man Song" rings out
and cradles us
in naked suits of Nova Scotia down-home
tears and hearts
even, fleetingly, two Calgary-come-lately cowboys
dazed by the symphony of silence
which accompanies the waves of
"The Working Man Song"
as it pours over us
daytime teacher, lawyer, business skins gone
it's all just a smokey Lord Nelson barroom
a Big Pond lady
and us becoming Rita.

we are all you in the bell of your voice
songs of love and struggle
songs of heart and home
long years of Cape men underground fill a smokey room
as the bell of your voice rings out
and we're all becoming Rita.

30

Phillips Square 18/08/83

under a hot Montreal sky
wrapped in the
unrelenting arms and charms of
cette belle ville
a crazy old man walking towards us
saying:
      "No smiles.
      there are no smiles in there."
so I gave him one
and; looking at the two Quebecois I am with,
I agree
and commiserate with my smile
too late
he is already retreating
offering the same plea to the pigeons
      "No smiles.
      There are no smiles in there."
his lunacy,
his chatter makes me smile
too bad he's too lost in his own mystic to see it
and, *lunacy* being so correct
in the hot arms of this
sun-lust lady-city called Montreal
on the even of the
Chinoise Fete de Gateau de la Lune

immediately and completely,
I am taken away;

transported to the Phillips Square
of Leonard Cohen's poem

Leonard: the old men,
les vieux, are still there
letters of reference still crumbling in pockets
and, maybe speaking
all the languages of Montreal

but; as they sit and melt
    sit and look
    sit and wait
    sit and sit
ces hommes de Phillips Square
under the hot August Montreal sky
as hot as a lover's kiss

they do not speak the language of the crazy man's smile.

Curbside Dance

fifth of June
dance so cool
body leaned on carside
doing a curbside dance
hip into
leg into
foot into soul
sun beating down
in a slow Black
two-four doubletime of summertime
and the livin' is
fun work love easy
Black man
sun so fine
curbside dance
lean car body-fine
curbside dance.

Crazy Luce

For Lucy Mitchell, who died a one-hundred-year-old Black woman in 1910. She was known most of her adult life as "Crazy Luce", because of eccentric dress and behaviour in the streets. But she surely was somebody's sweet child once, and probably wanted to be somebody's lover, friend, wife, and mama.

Crazy Luce.
Crazy Luce. Who are you?
Who are you?
Who are you, Black woman called crazy?
Crazy Luce
frozen on a page dated 1880
frozen in the Nova Scotia Archives
looking, sounding
written for all the world to see as crazy
yet; looking, sounding
written up as any woman, person, man,
person of stage, screen, play, dance
entertainment!
your carnival game/life/world
of living
crazy in your music-loving dress
crazy in your crazy hat
crazy in your crazy ways

did you laugh with no teeth?
did you roll/flash white eye?
did you shimmy-shuffle
body/bum wave

wiggle shuckjive dance
broken man-boot footed
clanging tambourine jangle?

did you paint the air fore and aft
with your wild rosehip
burdock bush, tansy tea
months of same clothes
same dress over dress over dress
warm mossy woman smell?

no luxury of hot bath waiting
no luxury of time for
no luxury of wanting to
no luxury of needing to
be crazy luce crazy luce crazy luce crazy luce crazy

generations earlier,
in white, white, whiter skin, and man-body
you would have been an artful and
cherished player on some bard's boards...
in my time
if you had descended time's ladder
in my time
you would be Diana Ross, Moms Mabley, Pearl Bailey
sequins, Broadway, Johnny Carson, *Ebony Magazine* fine
but in your poor, poor Black self and lifetime
frozen on a page dated 1880
from the Nova Scotia Archives of stark remnants of Blackpast
you are crazy, Luce.
Black and crazy, Luce.
Crazy Luce.

Reach Out and Touch

baby girl, baby boy behind me on the bus
reach out
and touch the curly electric of my hair
your fingers dipped in the
brown skin magic of my neck
to see if it comes off
your mama
slapping hands away
hush-up of your questions
and wondering out loud
why it doesn't come off.
I turn and smile for you,
but you're already lost
in the silence and the fear that motherlove wraps you in.
I should have sat beside you
snugged my big warm self up close
held you while your mama juggled parcels.
then you would know it's o.k.

The Profile of Africa

we wear our skin like a fine fabric
we people of colour
brown, black, tan coffeecoffee cream ebony
beautiful, strong, exotic in profile
flowering lips
silhouette obsidian planes, curves, structure
like a many-shaded mosaic
we wear our skin like a flag
we share our colour like a blanket
we cast our skin like a shadow
we wear our skin like a map
chart my beginning by my profile
chart my beginning by my colour
read the map of my heritage in
my face
my skin
the dark flash of eye
the profile of Africa.

Edith Clayton's Market Baskets

Edith Clayton
brown basket lady
from years past
shoppers carrying finely crafted bits of you
home with them
good maple wood-woven in
stripped with ancient craft
brown hands-woven in
a piece of Preston woods-woven in
little-girl years of watching-woven in
the weaving at an old Black gramma's hands-woven in
to market, to market, to market
over an eclipse of years-woven in
long forgotten and home in Preston
now days
babies/baskets/heart and soul-woven in.

Edith Clayton woven in
dust years of Black Africa-woven in
shoppers
they don't see or know or feel
the weight of who you are, Edith
from some dark Africa woman
weaving years gone by
shoppers
carrying bits of you away
in finely crafted maple baskets
from Preston woods.

But, do I know you
and claim you, as I should?
as you urge me to
gentle brownblack warm mother-eyes
ancient dust Africa hands
weaving baskets

"Come chile," you said
"Years are going round and round like my baskets."

Edith Clayton
I am like your children
owning you with my eyes on your craft
your name singing from my lips to newcomers:
Edith Clayton's market baskets
Will I "come chile and learn?"
Will I sit in the embrace of
some long-ancient dust Africa woman
good maple wood
going round and round
weaving years of Black living into baskets
will I let the craft live on in me
in my hands
will I be ancient and brown
haunting the Preston wood for good maple
Edith Clayton
Africa years in baskets.

Baobab Journey

In all of Africa, for all time, the baobab tree has been comfort, shelter, food, drink, mother, and life to Black African peoples. This poem is for her, the baobab; for all that she has witnessed, and for all that she has been.

the far reluctant journey
we have come
this long, vast baobab journey
boabab distance from Blackpast
mother Africa distant;
tree-breasted plain
Zambesi river basin
long moan
down the dark passage
of slave master
torrent rain of
terror
driven far past tree, baobab tree
baobab tree motherland
long gone Serengeti dreams.

Black Heritage Photos: Nova Scotia Archives

whose wedding day?
whose Black Loyalist shack?
whose shuffle, bone-weary
going down the road
laden, to market:
Bishop's Row
frost-bite
morning cold dreams
from "New Road"
    Africville
    down the line
    to town
into service
old dreams
yours
mine
and all of us.

Borrowed Beauty

we've come full circle
from turban/headed women (hiding cornrows)
in servitude; cooking
        suckling
        cleaning
everlasting   cleaning
        cooking
        suckling
        cleaning
from turban-headed women (hiding cornrows)
to precious, time-driven 'dos
to free-form Afros
nocturnal braids escaping into
beautiful, magical,
free-flying cloud Afros at
dawn, dusk, midnight
to our cornrows earning some woman named "10"
magic money in flickers of
light and colour.

Do you know, Africa's child, woman,
black brown tan;
with our corn rows?
you are nobody's beauty but our own
and named Sahara, Zaire, Zimbabwe, Cairo,
Nefertiti, Cleopatra or Nigeria.

this is no borrowed beauty,
this is home.

Black Teacher: To This World, To My Students

take my grandfather
three, four, five times removed
the true distinction of that denied me:
history's blank pages;
unwilling transplant to some distant shore
trailing lineage
scarred with battle
royal with kingship; or
dust-weary with nomadage;
the blurred and nebulous facts
now arrange themselves
here
in Africa's face, child, manhood, mother
woman
here on this shore.

take my father
strong,
fibrous tree-trunk of a man
leonine;
a pride of children
his legacy;
a footnote to those desperate, blank pages.

take my mother
indestructive;
a true testimony to:
behind every Black man

there stands the image of Black woman
                    mother
                    proud
                    strong
                    fighting
                    caring

reaching out for the future
grasping it defiantly for her children
defying and denying the ravages of
time's artful and awesome challengers of her Black strength.

take me
Africa's face upturned to the world
having plumbed empty chapters
having turned the page
having traded on the denial
                    the sacrifice
                    the pain of the fathers' fathers

take me as a true Black statement
take me as a legacy of the fathers
take me as a witness
for I demand to read every word
and to write some of my own.

The Top Street

"on the *top street*" was one of Daddy's sayings
"stay off the *top street*."
What was there?
If I was here, where was there?
this 'top street' that used to be Commercial Street, in Dartmouth
a good, practical Loyalist name.

someone married you,
top street of my down home,
downtown Dartmouth little Black girl years;
someone,
some mayor,
someone married you to parking lot status;
shorn you of your stately turn-of-the-century charm
and called you Alderney Drive.

Family Portrait

that little gallery on my wall
you
staring out at me from
long Tynes
　　　Tynes
　　　Tynes years past:
my daddy (now dead) at 7 or 10
his mama Nellie
so much like me
and all of my sisters.
I walk down my hallway
seeing, and not seeing her with
my eyes
my lips
my apple-cheeks in smile
I am her namesake.

I see and not see
grandma Nellie in period Loyalist dress
and great-grandma Mary
all starched apron white-white-white
great-grandfather Thomas
(my brother Pete in now-days)
in stiff black stuff
staring straight ahead,
defying the lens like a cadaver.

the background
now, old-photo cracked,
is my homestead house
white-washed
with cast-iron cookpans hung
like slave quarters

the start of the girlhood home of
my North Street Dartmouth youth
my beginning.

old photo gallery,
I love you
and I see you
and, I don't.

Now I See You

(poem for my mother; Ada Maxwell Tynes)

When did I start looking at you, my mother?
I don't know;
but often, it's your hands I'll watch
all brown, and bumpy-smooth
those same hands that
held and cradled me,
in my new life.

I look at your nose,
so high and strong, for a Black woman;
the same nose of
some noble African tribe. But where? Where?

I look at your eyes.
They've seen so much. So much.
You'll never tell me.

The hardest look of all
was the one I took of you sleeping.
and, missing my dad, still;
you lie with pillows piled high
and nestled close beside you, in sleep.

You Don't See Me

she nodded
old grey head soft, and full of
"Who's your mama?"
"Where you from, gal?"
I nodded back
giving her my best "I'm Joe Tynes' girl" smile

too many black brown
tan
coffeecoffee cream eyes
not sharing the light;
can't count heads nodding
on Barrington Street these days.
Don't you know,
sweet brown thing,
fine Black man,
hurry-footed for banking, lawyering,
teaching, trucking, selling,
dancing, loving
it's our eyes saying hello
and hugging a black and perfect stranger with your heart
it's saying, yes, I'm here, and
I'm glad you are, too;
who's making it, or
breaking their souls and backs in this life
is not at issue;
it's an old and Black way of chasing fears,
and old, old devils;

sharing life, and
ties that bind, timelessly
in colours rich in darkness.

Love - Route

you
me
the "we" of us
suspended in time
until here and now
ravelled and unravelled
in the labyrinth of time
travellers
on the many-chanelled route
of love
of time
divergent
dovetailed
day
minute
hour
life/time
ours now
the "we" of us
defying the labyrinth
of life and time and love

fingers of time stretched until they
caught us
travelling, travelling, travelling
you and I
under ever-changing skies
and clouds and suns

that knew our destiny
and winds that took us there
to a place where
as lovers in a strange and distant land
there were no eyes but ours
to see each touch
to count each drowning kiss
only the whispering silence of
travelling, travelling, travelling
the soft black velvet night of you
    soft black velvet nights with you
nights that glitter gold-black
flamingo passion and
cooling the hot-cool of lapis lazuli delight
of night and day and night
of you
of we
and of us
jazz
like jazz like jazz
Billie Holiday, Bessie Smith
Alice Walker, Alberta Hunter
jazz/woman delight of love
and loving
man/woman jazz
jazz
jazz
jazzing
the cool sweet blue-black jazz-dance
of love
of man and wife/woman and man/and life

the jazz of honeymoon hands across the pillow
        of honeyman hands across the pillow
        colouring this day of days
        this wedding day
with the ancient Fulani, Mandinka, Hausa
                Zulu, Zambesie, Shona
jazz/love music of hands
clapping the rhythm of love
'til only the lovers' hands
rejoice in making that joyful noise
joyful joy
joy of life and loving
joy of man/woman
out of Africa Queen mother woman
and into you
            me
the "we" of us
on this ancient and many-channelled
route of love.

En Route

(For Bob Bradford, July, 1985 at 35,000 feet)

we connect
through the unspoken airport language of
lines and waiting
and the public intimacy of security checks
you, walking through
man-stride strong, and forward
to door "0"
which does not yield
you enter my space
cameras erect
man-stride strong, and forward
we connect
through the eerie
eye-skin-mind-to-mind language of journalists
wordsmiths
writers en route
we connect
the mind-dance begins and plays in earnest;

in a far corner, but ear-distant
two mutes miss their plane
and flail the air
in the media-familiar, Middle Eastern forearm thrust of anger
and bawl a wordless violence
but up close, we speak
and if I could say that you were light on your feet,

I would
but we speak the word-dance of writers en route
a litany of
your commitments and mine
your world view and mine

Air India
and customs
pre and post-Shiite Beiruit
close calls and close-ups
luggage
and lenses
your assignments and mine

I wrote you into my book of en route wonders.

speaking the language
in those airport moments
we are close
as the intimacy of lovers
the gauntlet of travel by air married us that way
from Toronto to Halifax
then,
LIFE magazine
Saturday Evening Post, goodbye.

Vincent Knew The Colour Of Pain

I need the hot blue
VanGogh crazy passion
gold-yellow in my eyes
colouring my sight of you
in my head
in my bed
in and out and in my life
they thought he was crazy
Vincent, he was in love
crazy in love
crazy in life
crazy in colour
lived in canvas and colour
ate in the truth of it
what his eyes saw
between the lines of real life
breathed out those
mad passion hot gold swirls of
suns and starry nights and
deep blue sea skies over
rolling thunder cornfields
cut off his ear for love
you cut out my heart
squeeze it on a canvas
Vincent would approve
our own starry night of
suns and wildflowers
can throb and writhe

in a pigment of passion and colour
reach one finger into my eye
twist it, Picasso-like
onto the canvas made from the
bedsheets of our last coupling

Vincent will not mind.
he knows how long I have
loved and understood him
not crazy,
just in love.

became a hollow-man for love
gaunt and deep black-eyed
ascetic of face
and neck and hand

they say
you wanted paints and brushes and
went all pigmenty-fingered to the end

Ah, Vincent
such courage for love
such crazy hot-blue and
passion-gold courage for love
because we love and understand, you and I
colour me some of that
knife-edge in the heart of love
courage
as my soul chases down the
devil in that man
who squeezes my heart onto canvas

plays in it
rolls around in my heart
eats it
eats it
eats it like a lover
tears off the canvas
laughing like the joker in
every deck of cards
every deck
stacked back-to-back
like some trick and broken ladder

the canvas doesn't work for him
rolls and twists it
my heart smashed and oozing
that hot and screaming pigment
through the folds.

gone now
forgotten in someone's garbage
like Vincent's ear.

Lost and Found

found someplace
deep inside of me
some deep, black place
way beyond the woman-place of me
deep and deep and deep
buried you there
buried your name
buried the heart and soul
and face of you
buried your eyes that saw me as woman
before anyone else
before any man
buried your lips that
did and said and kissed
away all of the firstness of me
buried those hands
   those hands
   those hands
   those hands
they gave my passion language
and life
and made my soul sing long ago
and cry out your name
in love
buried that man-thing
that taught me the song of passion
and the joy of
man-woman-jigsawpuzzle

hand-in-glove fitting together
buried the smell
    the sight
    the sound of you
    the ghost of your touch
    the salt and dreams of
you in me, and
you and me
buried your name
buried your name
buried your name.

Annapolis Royal Crowning: January, 1985

Daureen Lewis
first mayor
female
and Black
chains of office adorning
your chest
so heavy
like some long-ago Zambezi-woman's
breastplate
or Ubangi-madonna neck-coil
do you wear your shield of office and firstness
less proud
as you smile and weave away
your status
the Black first womanliness
of you
as you stand
in this light and shadow
quirk of heart of darkness 1985?

Halifax-Dartmouth Ferry

1. The Boat Walk

people
from cars and buses,
taxis and long walks
approaching the ferry building:
the full-bodied run/trot of
young women and men
the pace of youth raising chests
chests raising coats
hair afly as they canter forward
abreast the executive striding
and women of a certain age
taking careful steps
huddled in mufflers for warmth
and last decade's fur, for style
against the early morning
Dartmouth harbourside cold.

2. The Ride Back

the ride back to Dartmouth
by ferry
the best part,
chorus of
train
train
train

train
train
on the Dartmouth side.

my breast in the window-mirror,
partridge-round,
well bound in mock Siberian woman reflection
against the cold
and from the real world
of 6:00 a.m. radio info gab/talk

a crest of sun reflecting back eye-winks
into the Cole Harbour abyss of ism.

3. -19° C, 8:00 a.m. Ferry Ride

ice on the harbour
scarlet flash of nail
on front seat
red-hat woman
herring-boned against
March 7 Halifax Harbour cold
ferry boat ride.

a long/short cruise of
oil rig
eerie Dartmouth fog skyline
sister-boat
riding crest of hoar-frost wave
brave upper-deck souls in sight.

4. Sharing the Ride

unknown, unnamed sister/woman on board
your head, three-quarters turned to me
your wild doe eye
framed by herring-bone collar,
fringe of hair,
arch of brow, and
tamed by Lancome
        Elizabeth Arden
Revlon Sable Brown mascara-spiked eye envied
by scalp of some moonlight Barrington Street-corner
punk man
punk woman.

5. Gulls and Ducks, -18° C, 7:45 a.m.

how can they sit
and float
and bob like that
gulls white-breasted, and
black duck dinners
outside my ferry-window
on this frigid Halifax Harbour morning crossing
perhaps their dovetailed and water-proof bottoms
are warmed by the pink and growing
fingers of eastern dawn
or, like mine
much better warmed by
nights and
mornings and
thoughts of you.

The Bay

you must have known my soul
Christopher Pratt
when you painted the Bay
for when I stand before it
the blues well up and lap around me
in a wash of joy and comfort and the pure
wonder of wonder
of sea and sky and heart and mind
and the wonder of me
as I stand, suddenly alone
dwarfed by, and
drawn to, and
compelled by
the blues, the blues, the blues of
the Bay
and, standing there,
your Bay is all that I need
feeling that blue-pigment breeze of sea and sky
feeling the blues
I am your horizon
and your waves and waves and waves
and all of your sky
standing there
your Bay is all of my thirst, my hunger, my desires
and fills and answers me
as no man ever has.

Chameleon Silence

I feel very Indian tonight
very Micmac
    Kuakiutl
    Huron
and Black
my tongue growing back 200, 500 years.
I speak in beauty
the truth of earth and sky
virgin breath of
who I am
what I feel.

you don't hear the roots and leaves
of my words
hanging like black veins from my lips
you clip the hedge
and build a railway through the field and rock
and stream of my words
like your three-times gone grandaddy did
under this maple sky.

tonight this Black woman sleeps on
the blood-carpet of broken treaty-dreams of long ago.

But this is 1985.
And tonight I know,
like a maidenhead just gone
why, Indian woman,
you are me.

Two People Openly Lighting Up Cigarettes

two people openly lighting up cigarettes
a young man lighting first,
then,
leaning in to the young woman beside him
lighting her;
she, tossing back auburn mane of hair
that just so sophisticated thrust of head
so easily read across the room
both, inhaling deeply
the heave and sigh of breast
and chest and
exhale of smoke of the long first drag
a charade of ritual and pleasure;
two people openly lighting up cigarettes
in that autumn Writers' Federation Salon room;
defying the new norm
inhaling deeply
to disappear by degrees
going up in smoke.

In Service II

In Service. I grew up hearing those words. As a little girl in my mother's kitchen, I would hear those words. In Service.

"She went In Service."

With little-girl ears where they shouldn't be, bent to lady-talk. That scary, hushed, exciting lady-talk between my mother and women who came to see her. Tea and talk. Lady-talk.

In Service. Mama and Miss Riley. Mama and Aunt Lil. Mama and Helen. Helen. The one grown-up person we were allowed to say the name of without a Miss or Aunt in front. Helen. I love to say her name and feel her velvet hats. Tams. She always chewed Juicy Fruit gum.

It was always the same. Talk of dark and mysterious women-things, softly spoken. Lips would burble tea in cups. Eyes would roll slowly or point sharply when certain things were said, names were named. Sometimes talk of Mama's In Service memories; of her grandmother, a ten year old girl being sent in from the country, from Preston, to be In Service. Talk of Aunt Lil, and, sometimes with her. Laughing Aunt Lil, with hair like fleeting movie star dreams. Aunt Lil who always included laughing in her lady-talk. And Miss Riley, who never did.

These conversations always seemed to carry their own colours. This one - scary, smoky black, light misty grey. Lady-talk. "Children should be seen and not heard." "Keep in a child's place." I was afraid of those hard, red sentences Mama always had ready during lady-talk. I had to go where they couldn't see me. But in a small house, the scary grey black mist of lady-talk can always find you.

In Service. Sterling silver, glowing in the dark - and - sunlight words to me. Like the lone brass button always at the bottom of Mama's button box, when I would sneak the polish to it, to bring back the shine. The Mysteries of In Service were all confused and glowing with parade dreams and uniforms marching by in a flash of things shiny and formal.

"Yes, girl, she went In Service when she was ten."

"It was right after I went In Service that Uncle Willy died."

"She was In Service for years."

"She died In Service."

My little-girl mind imagined shiny, wonderful things, not clearly defined. Not knees sore from years on hardwood floors. Not hands cracked, dry and painful, calloused and scrubworn. Not early morning walking miles into town to start the day off right with morning labours for some family. Not always going to and coming from the back door. Not "speak when you're spoken to," see and don't see, hear and don't hear, in case you anger them and they let you go. Not eating their leftovers in the kitchen alone. Not one dollar a day for back-breaking floors, walls, dishes, furniture, windows, washing, ironing, sweat-soaked labour. In Service.

"She died in service." That describes Helen. I was allowed to say her name. Velvet tams and Juicy Fruit gum every night in Mama's kitchen. When I was little, I was allowed to stand by her and feel her tams. When I got older, she'd be there every night, watching me cry into cold dishwater.

And still the tams were there. The ruby, the emerald green, the midnight velvet blue of them glowed richly against the grey-black, soft and woolly head. Sometimes she would reach up, too, to finger that soft glow; almost as if to make sure that lovely part of her was still there. Helen's hands against such splendid velvet were like wounds; flags of the world of drudgery that were her days.

Helen was someone's girl, this never married Black lady, already in middle age by the time I was old enough to know her. Somebody's girl. Not in the romantic notion of being somebody's girl (friend). Helen was some white lady's girl; some white family's girl. She came to our house every night as if it was a target; an end point to her day; to sit in our kitchen with a cup of tea; to read the paper. She never took her coat off.

The lady-talk would start. Mama and Helen. It was always about Helen's lady - the woman she worked for. "My family." My Missus."

Helen "lived In Service," which added to the mystique of it all. My little-girl mind imagined something with a faint glow. Not a room off the back. Not living away from your family. In a house, a bed that was never yours.

Through my window, I could see "Helen's house" not far from my own. On Sunday walks with one or other of my older sisters, seeing "Helen's house" was to see a dream, or at least a story-book page. "Helen's house," huge and golden yellow, with a fence and a yard that held what, in later, grown up years, I would know as a gazebo. But then, surely, that wonderful little in-the-yard house was where she lived, behind cool, dark green lattice. Helen's house. So different from my own, so squat and brown and hen-like. My house; teeming with the dozen of us. My house, that Helen fled to each night; to maybe, for a little while, be a little of what my mother was, and did and had. Mama, with hands on her own dishes; on her own child.

Helen had eyes that were always friendly. I would see them peek behind her tam, even as she sat, and sipped her tea, and waited for it all to happen every night. Waited in the wake of the dark and tiny storm of activity that hummed along after Mama; a whirl-wind of shooing the creeping horde of us; of moving through clouds of flour from baking; of ironing, of putting up late supper for Daddy; of watching and listening for Daddy; and finally settling down to braid my hair and have tea and lady-talk.

Sometimes Helen would bring a shopping bag full of clothes with her to show Mama. Clothes — castoff, not new — that her lady had given her. Clothes and hats. Velvet tams. Helen. Mama and Helen and lady-talk.

What did a little Black girl know, touching a velvet tam over hooded and frightened eyes? Helen. Perhaps she knew and feared the loneliness of her own life, circled round and round her like an echo; loneliness circled round and worn close, fitting her like the coats and tams from her shopping bag. Perhaps the secret mystery and the fear should hide deep in her eyes from me; from my little-girl eyes watching Helen bring the secret of In

Service each night. This world, this life, this loneliness all too real for her. A dark and female mystery still for me.

Helen. Driven like a magnet to somebody else's kitchen; somebody else's child. Helen. With care-worn hands, handing me the future luxury of dreams, and thoughts, and "I remember Helen," and the awful mystery of In Service unravelled now from the whispers of lady-talk, found now in the voice of these words.

Looking back, I know she was saving me. They all were. Helen. Mama. Miss Riley. Aunt Lil. My sisters. Known and unknown Black women. Armies of Black women in that sea of domestic service. With unlikely and unowned addresses. Waiting for buses on prestigious street corners. Carrying back bits and remnants of that other world of In Service in shopping bags; and wearing the rest in coats and velvet tams.

Maxine Tynes is a writer who has lived, studied, and worked all of her life in Dartmouth, Nova Scotia. Her heritage goes back to the time of the Black Loyalists in Nova Scotia. Maxine is a graduate of Dalhousie University in Halifax, and is currently a member of the board of governors at Dalhousie, the first Black Nova Scotian to hold this appointment.

Ms. Tynes is a freelance broadcaster with CBC Radio. She has co-written and performed in a docu-drama based on the death of Stephen Biko, a Black anti-apartheid freedom-fighter in South Africa. Her poetry and prose has appeared in literary publications and on CBC's "Anthology". She is well known for her numerous and lively poetry readings. While a student at Dalhousie, Maxine won The Dennis Memorial Poetry Prize.